American Government Today

YOUR
RIGHT TO VOTE

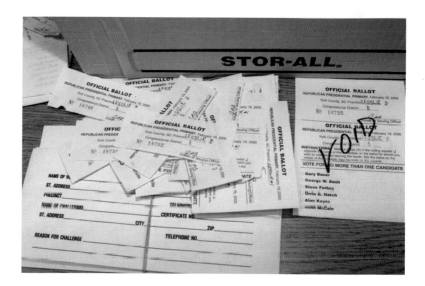

By Mark Sanders

STECK-VAUGHN
ELEMENTARY · SECONDARY · ADULT · LIBRARY

A Harcourt Company

www.steck-vaughn.com

Printed and bound in China
10 9 8 7 6   788 05

Photo Acknowledgments
Cover ©CORBIS/Catherine Karnow; p.1 ©Chuck Burton/AP/Wide World Photos; p.4a ©Eric Gay/AP/Wide World Photos; p.4b ©Doug Mills/AP/Wide World Photos; p.7 ©AP/Wide World Photos; p.11 ©Jay Laprete/AP/Wide World Photos; p.15a ©AP/Wide World Photos; p.15b ©Allan Tannenbaum/SYGMA; p.16 ©Stevan Morgain/AP/Wide World Photos; p.19 ©JL Atlan/SYGMA; p.20 ©Jim Cole/AP/Wide World Photos; p.24 ©Spencer Tirey/AP/Wide World Photos; p.26a ©Doug Mills/AP/Wide World Photos; p.26b ©David J. Phillip/AP/Wide World Photos; p.29 ©Doug Mills/AP/Wide World Photos; p.30 ©Seanna O'Sullivan/AP/Wide World Photos; p.33 ©Rhonda Simpson/AP/Wide World Photos; p.35 ©Wesley Wong/AP/Wide World Photos; p.41 ©Eric Draper/AP/Wide World Photos.

CONTENTS

Introduction   5

The Importance of Voting   6

Becoming a Voter   8

The Right to Vote   10

Political Parties   13

Choosing Candidates   17

Primaries   21

National Conventions   23

Campaigns   27

Election Day   31

The Electoral College   36

Beyond the Voting Booth   40

Glossary   44

Index   47

INTRODUCTION

When people are 18 they usually are able to vote in a U. S. election. However, even people who are not yet 18 are probably voting. They may be voting for a class president in school. Or perhaps they are voting for a leader at their church or temple. They also may be voting when their family needs to make decisions.

This book tells you what you need to know about voting. You will see how candidates, or the people running for office, are chosen. You will learn about the election process. You will also find out why your vote is important. Learning about these things will help make you a well-informed voter.

(Top) George W. Bush, a Republican, and (bottom) Al Gore, a Democrat, were the leading candidates in the 2000 presidential election.

5

THE IMPORTANCE OF VOTING

Voting is one of the most important rights of U.S. citizens. Through voting they are able to choose the officials who will lead or represent them.

Voting is the starting point of democracy, because in a democracy, the people elect representatives. This is because it is not possible for each citizen to take part directly in the work of government. Representatives are directing the government on the part of the citizens who elect them. These citizens are known as constituents. Elected officials represent their constituents' needs and concerns. However, they also become involved in political matters that will affect all citizens.

People vote for candidates who will represent them at all levels of government. More than one-half million Americans are elected to the jobs they hold in local, state, and national governments.

Bill Clinton was elected the 42nd president of the United States.

 6

BECOMING A VOTER

All citizens of the United States may be able to vote. However, not everyone living in the United States can vote. In order to vote, a person must meet certain requirements. For one thing, he or she must be a U.S. citizen. Anyone born in the United States is a citizen. Also, children born to U.S. citizens who live outside the United States are U.S. citizens from birth.

Aliens, or natives of foreign nations who live in the United States, are not permitted to vote. This is because they are not citizens. Once they have become citizens, they may be able to vote in all elections.

There are other conditions that a person must meet as well. In order to vote, citizens must be at least 18 years old. In some cases they must show that they can read and write. They must also have lived in their area for a certain period of time. This period may be a year or several months, depending on the laws in the area.

Citizens can have their right to vote taken away if they have been arrested for a serious crime, or if they are said to be mentally unfit.

To vote, a person must first register. People register to vote by putting their names on the list of qualified, or approved, voters in their communities. People usually register to vote at the town hall or city hall where they live. They may also register in public libraries, shopping malls, or civic centers. All states require people to register before they can vote except the state of North Dakota.

THE RIGHT TO VOTE

In the early days of the country, not many Americans were allowed to vote. Over time, this has changed. Often the change took place in the form of an amendment, or change, to the U.S. Constitution. This document lists all of the basic laws of the United States.

At that time, only white male landowners were allowed to vote. After the Civil War (1861-1865), the 15th Amendment to the Constitution gave African-American men the right to vote. This amendment outlawed treating people differently because of their race. Women were given the right to vote in 1920 when the 19th Amendment was passed.

In 1924 Congress passed a law giving Native Americans the right to vote. Citizens of Washington, D.C., did not have the right to vote in presidential elections until 1961. In 1961 the 23rd Amendment to the Constitution changed this.

There have been other amendments as well that have changed some voting rules. In 1964, the 24th Amendment outlawed poll taxes. These were fees that

This girl has come with her mother to the voting place.

people had to pay before they could vote. These fees kept the poor and less educated from voting.

Until 1971, U.S. citizens had to be 21 in order to vote. The 26th Amendment lowered the age to 18. Mostly this was due to America being part of the Vietnam war. Young men who were only 18 could be drafted to serve in the armed forces. Because of this, many people felt 18-year-olds should be allowed to vote. It took only three months and seven days for the amendment to be approved.

Puerto Rico is a commonwealth of the United States. This means that although it is united with the United States, it governs itself. The people there enjoy many of the rights and privileges of U.S. citizens. But they cannot vote in presidential elections.

POLITICAL PARTIES

Voting is only half of the election process. The other part involves the people who are running for office.

Most people who run for public office belong to a political party. A political party is made up of a group of individuals who share the same basic political views. A political party tries to get its members elected so that the party can control the government.

In the United States, there are two main political parties, the Democrats and the Republicans. The Democratic party usually feels the federal government should help solve problems in the nation. The Republican party usually believes state and local governments should deal with the nation's problems.

Some people do not belong to either of the two major political parties. They are known as Independents. These people believe that some views of both parties make sense. In elections, they may vote for Republican or Democratic candidates. Or they may choose candidates from smaller political parties.

Political parties help their candidates in several ways. Parties have ties with people who are already in office. These people may talk up the person who is running for office. Parties also have supporters in business and in the community who may be willing to donate, or give, money to help the candidate get elected.

Parties have the power and money to set up rallies. These are meetings that are held in order to stir up excitement for the party's candidate. Parties also talk about their candidate's message in telephone calls as well as on radio and television.

In addition, parties print and pass out booklets, posters, and campaign buttons to try to interest voters in their candidate.

The elephant (top) has long been the symbol of the Republican party. The donkey (below) stands for the Democratic party.

CHOOSING CANDIDATES

How do political parties come up with their candidates? Where do the names of candidates come from? If a person is interested in running for office, he or she makes this known by talking with party leaders and by giving speeches to groups of people. Usually, the next step is to collect the names of thousands of people on a petition. A petition is a paper asking for something. In this case, it asks a party to make the person an official candidate. The more names the petition has, the more popular the person is.

Next, the person must find money in order to run. People may give money to a candidate. If they do this, it shows that a candidate can get enough money to win an election.

After this, the candidate needs nominations by leaders in the political party. This means that the party leaders suggest the candidate for office.

Running for office costs a great deal of money.

Often, committees within a party come up with the names of possible candidates. To do this they talk to people already in the government. They may also talk to people from the world of sports and entertainment. These people may be interested in running for office, and they are already known to the public.

The best example of a famous person who ran for office is Ronald Reagan. He was a popular actor who first became governor of California and then president. The party may also look for someone who has already held some kind of public office. Often success in a lower level office helps a candidate move up to a more important position.

President Reagan welcomes President Cerezo of Guatemala to the White House.

A worker writes down the total number of votes for candidates in the 2000 New Hampshire primary.

PRIMARIES

Sometimes, as many as six or eight candidates from the same political party may want to run for the same office. Primary elections help the parties find out which candidates have the best chances of winning a general election. Political parties hold primary elections to narrow down the list of candidates.

Primary elections, or primaries, are special elections among members of a political party to choose candidates to run for office in the name of their party. The candidate with the most votes is the party's nominee. A nominee is the person selected to run for office by his or her party. Primaries may be held any time during the year.

Almost from the country's beginning, some people did not like the idea of primary elections. Some argue that campaigning, or trying to win votes, for primary candidates is costly. They also think it is wasteful, since there is no promise that any of the candidates who win the primaries will win the election. In addition, few people vote in primaries, so the party's candidates are selected by only a small number of voters.

The first primary was held in 1842 in Crawford City, Pennsylvania. This election was to nominate, or select, candidates for a local election. Other places soon did the same for their own local elections.

By 1903 Wisconsin held the first primary to nominate candidates for state offices. By 1917 all but four states had made laws about primaries.

New Hampshire has the first presidential primary in the United States. The state law says that New Hampshire must hold its primary a week before any other state. For example, if Delaware is having its Republican primary on February 8, New Hampshire will have its primary on February 1. Other states schedule their primary elections soon after New Hampshire's.

NATIONAL CONVENTIONS

A convention is a large gathering of delegates. Delegates are people sent by local party branches from all over the country to act for them. Political parties hold conventions every year. But the largest ones take place in a presidential election year.

National conventions are held by political parties to officially choose their candidates for president and vice president. Before then, the candidates for vice president were chosen by the presidential candidates. Each party holds its own convention. Conventions are held in July and August of the election year.

Most of the convention activity is shown on national TV. Many people closely watch what goes on at the conventions. This may be their first close look at the candidates who will run for president.

Before the convention, nominating committees prepare a list of candidates. Many of these people have already won primary elections.

Party members also come up with a party "platform." This is a statement of the political party's position on important public issues. If elected, the candidate will base his or her actions on this platform.

Each stand on a certain issue is called a "plank" of the platform. Each political party's platform tries to win votes because a large number of people will agree with it. For example, a Democratic nominee for president might promise to end special tax breaks for big business. A Republican presidential nominee might promise that there would be no new taxes.

Posters, banners, signs with names and catchy slogans, and political buttons are all part of the convention process. They are another way that workers keep their candidates' names before the public.

Many speeches are made during the convention. These speeches stir up excitement about the party and its goals. Making speeches and introducing candidates at the convention can be a step to higher political careers for party workers. That is because the workers who make the speeches are seen and heard by people across the country.

Buttons are one way of letting the public know who the candidates are.

CAMPAIGNS

After a candidate is nominated at a national convention, he or she must organize a campaign. A campaign is a plan for winning votes for the party's candidate. A campaign needs to be good enough to get the person elected.

The first step in a campaign is to appoint a strong campaign manager. This person will be in charge of planning ways to win the coming election. One campaign strategy is to find ways to attract voters from certain key states—California, New York, Pennsylvania, Texas, Florida, and Illinois. These are the states with the highest populations and the largest number of votes.

During a campaign, the candidate must travel across the country so the public can get to know him or her better. Campaigning can be exhausting. Presidential candidates may fly or go by train to as many as eight or ten cities a day. They wave from cars or the backs of trains and they fly thousands of miles. Candidates must also go to many fund-raising dinners.

Candidates deliver many speeches during a campaign.

Polls are an important part of a campaign. These are surveys that measure the candidates' chances for winning an election. People are asked questions. Their answers are counted and the replies are made public. Polls are not sure things, but they do show general directions. They can also affect how the public thinks.

Studies have shown that elections are often personality contests. They are not only about political issues. Therefore, someone running for office wants to be seen as friendly and sincere. He or she also wants to appear calm when answering tough questions from journalists, newscasters, and members of the public. After all, a candidate needs to show that he or she can stand up to the pressures of office. To show a picture of family life, a candidate tries to appear in public with a spouse, parents, children—even a pet.

The news media play important roles in campaigns and elections. TV probably plays the biggest role. Showing campaigns as they are happening is a major media event. Millions of people watch speeches by candidates and powerful supporters on TV. Appearances on popular talk shows are another good way for a candidate to make his or her name and face familiar to the voting public.

During a campaign, the candidate tries to meet as many people as possible. He or she tries to meet people who are possible voters. Meetings with young people, even though they cannot vote, are also useful because they can help build support. Young people are often among the hardest campaign workers.

As Election Day nears, campaign volunteers become very busy. They try to make their candidate as well known as possible. They run advertisements on radio and TV and put ads in newspapers. They also try to make sure all the people who support their candidate will vote.

Al Gore (right) appears with Katie Couric on the popular "Today" show.

Curtains on voting machines give each voter privacy.

ELECTION DAY

Every year, the first Tuesday following the first Monday in November is Election Day throughout the United States. On that day, citizens take part in the work of democracy. On Election Day, voters elect all kinds of local and state officials. These officials may include governors, senators, representatives, mayors, school board members, and judges.

People may also vote for issues. Special issues called referendums are sometimes on the ballot. These ask voters to approve or disapprove changes to certain laws. Referendums may also ask about spending money for special projects, such as new roads or other public improvements.

On Election Day most people go to vote at an official polling place. Most polling places are in public buildings, such as schools or fire stations. Signs outside tell people that any kind of campaigning within a certain distance of the polling place is not allowed.

In most places, voters cast their votes using voting machines. Inside the voting machine, there is a list of the candidates. There may also be a description of the issues the voters are to decide. People cast their vote by pulling down a lever next to the candidate or issue they want to vote for.

In earlier times, election officials counted the number of votes for candidates by getting a spoken response that they marked down on a list. Voting machines were first used in 1892. In some smaller areas where it would be too costly to buy voting machines, paper ballots are still used. They are also used in cities when voters must cast an absentee ballot.

Absentee ballots are printed lists of the candidates mailed to voters. These voters request them because they will not be able to get to their polling places on Election Day. They may be away on business, vacations, or hospital stays. They may also be away at college or while serving in the armed forces. These people complete absentee ballots and mail them in.

The hours for voting change from state to state. In addition, there is a three-hour time difference between the East Coast and the West Coast. This means the polls

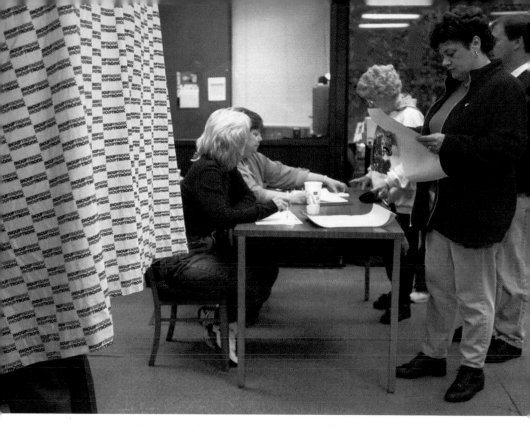

Voters in Kentucky review their official ballots while waiting in line to cast their vote.

in New York may close three hours before those in California. Because of these time differences, the result of an election may not be known and checked for several hours.

Within the next 50 years most voters may be able to cast their ballots by computer. Voters may vote from computers in their homes or offices. They will no longer have to visit a polling place. Many details will have to be worked out before electronic elections can be run smoothly. However, electronic reporting will certainly allow election returns to be counted almost immediately, as soon as the polls close.

Arizona Democrats started what they believe is the future of voting. In the Democratic presidential primary on March 7, 2000, they used the Internet. This became the nation's first on-line ballot cast in an election for public office.

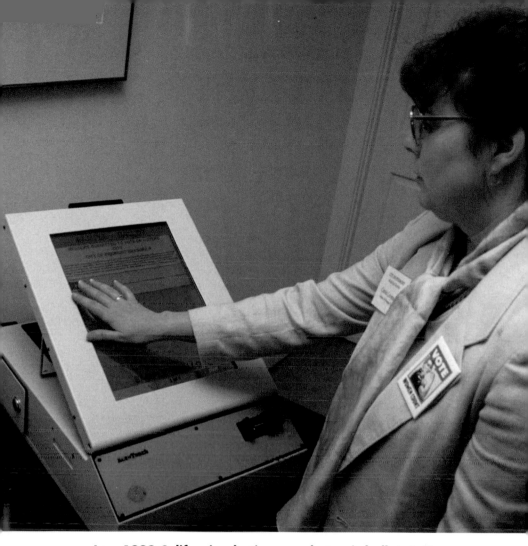

In a 1999 California election, an electronic ballot station was first used. It keeps a running total of votes cast.

THE ELECTORAL COLLEGE

When citizens cast their vote for the president and vice president, they are not really voting directly. They are actually casting a vote for an elector. An elector is a person chosen to represent the voter.

The writers of the Constitution set up the electoral college because they thought it would help democracy. They felt that people who did not know much about the candidates might elect an unsuitable person if everyone's vote counted directly. Therefore, the founders put the actual final choice of president into the hands of a group of electors. These electors look after the election of the country's presidential and vice presidential candidates.

Article 2, Section 1 of the Constitution directs the legislature of each state to choose its own electors. It lets the state governments decide for themselves how the electors will be appointed. Senators, representatives, and officers of the federal government may not serve as

 36

electors while they hold office. Members of the electoral college must cast their electoral votes to the candidate who has won the popular election in each elector's area.

The number of electors a state has in the electoral college is determined in the same way as the number of members of Congress from that state. Just as every state has two senators and a number of representatives based on that state's population, so every state has at least three electors. Several of the least populated states have only three. Alaska, Montana, Wyoming, North and South Dakota, Vermont, and Delaware are among these. The District of Columbia gets three electoral votes, even though it has no members in Congress.

There are currently 538 members of the electoral college. This is the same as the total number of senators and representatives in Congress. Since half of 538 is 269, 270 electoral votes are needed to show a clear majority.

The number of electors each state has can change, however. Every ten years the government counts the people in the United States. This is known as a census. The census tells how many people are living in the country and in which state they live. It also determines the number of electors each state has.

Congress counts the votes of the members of the electoral college on January 6, following the election. This is just a custom, however, because by this time plans have already been made for the president's inauguration. This is the ceremony in which the president takes the oath of office. This is set for the beginning of the fourth week in January.

In 1804 Congress ratified the 12th Amendment to the Constitution. This law requires electors to cast separate votes for presidential and vice presidential candidates. Although some people do not like the electoral college system, there are currently no plans to change it.

POPULAR VOTE V. THE ELECTORAL COLLEGE

Thirteen times in the history of the United States the electoral college has given the presidency to candidates who did not win a majority of the national popular vote. Most recently, Bill Clinton was elected in 1992 because of the electoral college, even though he did not have the majority of popular votes.

BEYOND THE VOTING BOOTH

Every four years people in the United States vote for a president. Citizens make what is probably their most important voting decision when they choose the person who will lead the country.

Generally, only slightly more than half of all registered voters have turned out for any of the presidential elections held since the 1920s. The 1960 presidential contest between Democrat John F. Kennedy and Republican Richard M. Nixon had the highest turnout, with just under 63 percent. This was also one of the closest elections.

Usually in local elections the turnout is 25 percent or less. Many people think that their votes don't count. But if everyone who is allowed to vote did vote, election results might be quite different.

These young people are learning to become involved in elections.

40

Although they cannot vote, it is important for minors, or people under the age of 18, to be involved. Minors also need representation in the government. Yet they cannot vote. Therefore, their concerns must be represented by advocates. Advocates are people who make sure that the needs of people are represented.

There are many ways for citizens of any age to take part in the political process. Know who is in government and who is running for office. Know why these people are in the positions they are. Work for the candidates. Other

The League of Women Voters is a national organization. The group gives free information to all voters. Its pamphlets and handouts tell about candidates' experiences. The group helps tell voters what candidates have done in the past. It also tell voters about candidates' stands on current issues.

ways to be involved are to respond to opinion polls, read and fill out questionnaires, and attend political rallies and meetings with members of government.

People can also take action on important issues. Anyone can take part in government by calling, writing, or E-mailing letters to members of Congress or other elected officials. Citizens of any age can express opinions. They can work to get the government to take action in a cause they believe in.

Become informed. Read newspaper stories about upcoming elections. Know the issues and where the candidates stand on them. Do not assume that the candidate with the most money to spend is necessarily the best candidate. One of the goals of education should be to prepare citizens to vote wisely.

Glosssary

Absentee ballots Printed lists of candidates used for voting by voters who are not able to get to their polling places on Election Day

Advocates Individuals who make sure that the needs of people are represented

Alien A person who lives in a country of which he or she is not a citizen

Amendment A formal change to the U.S. Constitution

Ballot A piece of paper used to cast a vote

Campaign A plan for winning votes

Candidate A person running for office

Census A count of the population

Citizen A person who is born in or who becomes a member of a specific country and, as a result, has the rights and privileges of that country

Convention A large meeting of delegates

Delegates Representatives of a political party who have been selected to choose candidates for office

Democracy A system of government in which the people govern by elected representatives

 44

Democratic party The U.S. political party that usually feels the federal government should solve problems in the nation

Election The act of deciding on a candidate or issue

Election Day The day that has been legally set aside for the election of public officials. In the United States, this is the first Tuesday following the first Monday in November.

Elector A person chosen to represent the voters

Electoral college A group of electors who oversee the election of the U.S.'s presidential and vice presidential candidates

Independents People who do not belong to either the Democratic or Republican party because they agree with some views from each party

Media Another name for the press

Nominee A party's candidate for office

Nominate To name a candidate to run for office

Petition A request signed by many citizens

Platform A party's position on important public issues

Political party A group of people who have similar ideas about government

Polls Surveys that ask questions of the public

Poll tax A fee a person had to pay before he or she could vote

Primaries Special elections among members of a political party to choose the candidates to run for office in the name of that party

Rallies Meetings held by a political party in order to stir up excitement for its candidate

Referendums Special issues put on the ballot for voters to decide upon

Register To put one's name on the list of approved voters in one's community

Representative A person who does the work of directing the government on the part of the citizens who elected him or her

Republican party The U.S. political party that usually believes the state and local governments, rather than the federal government, should deal with the problems in the nation

Vote A formal expression of opinion about a candidate or an issue

Index

absentee ballots 32
advocates 40
African Americans 10
aliens 8

ballot 31, 32, 33, 34

campaign manager 27
campaign workers 29
campaigns 21, 25, 27-29, 31
candidates 5, 6, 13, 14, 17,
    18, 21, 22, 23, 25, 27, 28,
    29, 32, 36, 39, 42, 43
census 37
citizen 5, 6, 8, 9, 31, 36, 40,
    43
Civil War 10
Clinton, Bill 39
committees 18
commonwealth 12
Congress 37, 38, 43
constituents 6
contributions 17
convention 23, 25, 27
Crawford City, Pa. 22

delegates 23
democracy 6, 31, 36, 40
Democratic party 13

Election Day 29, 31, 32
elector 36, 37, 38
electoral college 36-39
electoral votes 37, 38
electronic elections 34

15th Amendment 10
finances 17, 21

inauguration 38
Independents 13
Internet 34

Kennedy, John F. 40
key states 27

League of Women Voters 42

media, influence of 23, 28,
    29

national convention 23
Native Americans 10
New Hampshire primary 22
19th Amendment 10
Nixon, Richard M. 40
nominating committees 23
nomination 17
nominee 21

party leaders 17
petition 17
"plank" 25
"platform" 25
political party 13-14, 17, 18,
   21, 23, 25
poll taxes 10-11
polling places 31, 33, 34
polls 28, 32, 43
popular vote 39
presidential elections 10, 12,
   23, 27, 40
primary election 21, 22, 23,
   34
Puerto Rico 12

rallies 14, 43
referendums 31
Reagan, Ronald 18

registering to vote 9
representatives 6
Republican party 13

speeches 25

12th Amendment 38
24th Amendment 10
26th Amendment 11
23rd Amendment 10

U. S. Constitution 10, 36

Vietnam war 11
voting 5, 6, 8, 9, 10, 13, 31,
   32, 33, 34, 36, 40, 43
voting machine 32
voting requirements 8-9

Wisconsin primary 22
Women 10

young people, involvement
   in elections 5, 29, 42-43